Geopolitics in Virtual Reality

Visualizing Borders and Diplomatic Relations

Table of Contents

Chapter 1. Introduction

Immerse yourself in a world where complex geopolitical landscapes come alive, where borders aren't just lines on a 2D map, but rather represented in full spatial glory—welcome to our Special Report: "Geopolitics in Virtual Reality: Visualizing Borders and Diplomatic Relations." Delving into the never-before-seen nexus of politics and cutting-edge technology, we elegantly unravel the intricate dance of global diplomacy. With vivid portrayals of international divides, spatial renderings of political affiliations, and dramatizations of historical treaties, we make geopolitics not only easy to understand but fascinating to explore. Uncover the interactive potential of virtual reality, transforming how we comprehend and negotiate our world's knotty geopolitical contour. It's not your run-of-the-mill analysis—it's a passport to the future of international relations, and it's as enthralling as it is educational. So, get ready to be wooed by this technological marvel, and let's travel borders without leaving room, together!

Chapter 2. Geopolitical History Through a New Lens

So far, humanity's exploration of history has been limited to books, historical artifacts, movies, and other largely linear modes of understanding. With virtual reality (VR), we open up an unprecedented visual and immersive journey into the past, a tool that enables us to live through past events, rather than just reading about them. When applied to the subject of geopolitics, VR has the potential to transform entirely how we comprehend, experience, and engage with the past and the possibilities of the future.

2.1. Exploring Old Battles in New Ways

Consider, for instance, significant battles and conflicts that have shaped the geopolitical tapestry of our world. Through traditional means, we can read about the strategies employed, look at pictorial representations of the battlefield, and try to imagine the events unfolding. But with VR, we can make that leap from imagination to reality. We can virtually walk the grounds where the Battle of Waterloo was fought, see the soldiers' positioning, hear the cannon fires, and understand the tactical maneuvers made by both sides.

Not only does it make history more tangible, but it also allows us to appreciate and comprehend the strategic aspects and implications of these battles on the geopolitical landscape. Thus, it adds an extra dimension to our learning and enables us to empathize and connect with history like never before.

2.2. Visualizing Complex Geopolitical Transitions

Historical changes in territorial boundaries have often been the result of political machinations, wars, treaties, and diplomatic negotiations. Whole empires have been built and lost, impacting cultures, ethnicities, and economies.

Through VR, we can animate these changes as they happened over centuries. Instead of static maps, imagine watching the continent of Africa's political map morphing over a thousand years, its borders changing color and shape as empires rise and fall. We get to view the influence of colonial powers as they carve up the land among themselves, followed by the independence movements that reshape the map once again.

The movement from a two-dimensional plane to a three-dimensional representation changes the way these geopolitical shifts are perceived, making it easier to grasp the magnitude and impact of such changes.

2.3. Witnessing Diplomacy and Treaties in Action

VR brings treaties signed centuries earlier to life in your living room. It takes users back to the original settings of these diplomatic negotiations, enabling them to witness the verbal exchanges, arguments, and the eventual consensus-building which led to these historical decisions.

With VR, one could observe the Treaty of Westphalia's negotiations, ending the devastating Thirty Years' War in Europe and establishing a new balance of power. Dive into the tense atmosphere, see the players involved, and understand the delicate diplomatic dance that drew lines on maps and sowed the seeds for modern Europe.

2.4. A New Perspective on Impact of Development

Beyond mapping boundaries, VR can illustrate the political, social, and economic consequences of human actions. Users could see the effects of climate change in countries facing environmental challenges. They could observe shifting geopolitics driven by the hunt for scarce resources, migration trends, and new infrastructure projects such as China's Belt and Road Initiative. By visualizing these changes, VR could foster empathy and understanding, encouraging users to become more active global citizens.

2.5. Drawing the Future with VR

Looking forward, VR will change not only how we view the past, but also how we envision the future. As humanity ventures into uncharted territories like space exploration, climate change, and the proliferation of digital states, VR allows us to simulate various scenarios, anticipate potential geopolitical shifts, and plan accordingly.

The fusion of technology, politics, and history provides an innovative educational platform that caters to a new generation of learners, nurturing a more global, empathetic worldview and enabling a better understanding of the complex geopolitics navigated by leaders, diplomats, and citizens alike.

As this chapter has attempted to showcase, the intersection of VR and geopolitics promises a journey that is as illuminating as it is exciting. The potential of VR in reshaping our understanding is immense - it holds the power to push the boundaries of our collective imagination, and unlock a deeper, richer understanding of the world around us. In the end, VR isn't just a fresh lens to view geopolitics—it's a whole new paradigm.

Chapter 3. Understanding Virtual Reality: The Transformative Tech

To truly comprehend the transformative power of virtual reality (VR) technology, we must first unveil its intricacies, from its conception to recent advancements and applications. This technology, which remarkably transports users into an interactive 3D environment, is revolutionizing numerous sectors - entertainment, education, therapy, and now geopolitics, becoming an essential tool in visualizing and understanding complex global landscapes.

3.1. The Genesis of VR

Virtual reality, as an idea, isn't recently conceived, albeit, its concrete embodiment dappled the late 20th century. The concept traces back to the early 19th century with the introduction of panoramic murals – artworks designed to immerse the observer in a particular scene or event. However, it was in 1968 when tech pioneer Ivan Sutherland developed the first VR and augmented reality (AR) head-mounted display system, known as "The Sword of Damocles," considered the primal ancestor of modern VR technology.

The following decades experienced gradual progress, predominantly visible in the gaming industry with ventures like the Virtual Boy from Nintendo or Sega's VR Glasses. Unfortunately, limitations in technology and high costs stifled further advancement. The real breakthrough came well into this century, however, with enterprises such as Oculus Rift, HTC Vive, and later, Playstation VR, invigorating a new era of VR.

3.2. Grasping VR's Technical Base

To fully appreciate the influence this technology wields, a fundamental grasp of its underlying mechanisms is indispensable. At its core, VR operates by simulating our senses–sight, sound, and sometimes touch. This allows for the creation of an immersive environment that feels "real" to the user.

This is typically achieved through a combination of hardware and software components. A headset with one or two screens (one for each eye) displays a 3D-generated environment, convincingly creating an illusion of depth, while headphones provide spatial auditory input, adding to the experience's credibility. In more elaborate sets, additional equipment can be used to simulate tactile and even olfactory sensations.

3.3. Journey into the Realms of VR Applications

With an understanding of VR's mechanics, numerous applications are emerging beyond gaming and entertainment. Education is experiencing an overhaul, letting students explore ancient Roman streets or learn anatomy inside a virtual human body. Therapies exploiting VR for PTSD or acrophobia treatment usher in fresh possibilities for healthcare.

Companies have harnessed VR for training purposes, simulating scenarios that range from customer interactions for employees to intricate surgical procedures for doctors. The real estate industry leverages VR for virtual property tours, and architects use it to create spatial models of their blueprints.

However, the use of VR in the geopolitical sphere remains largely unexplored–until now. The application of VR in visualizing the geographical, social, and economic fabric of nations presents an innovative way of understanding the complex interplay between countries on the world stage.

3.4. Leveraging VR in Geopolitical Understanding

Imagine standing atop the Great Wall of China, then in mere seconds teleporting to the busy streets of Tokyo. Moments later, you are floating above the Panama Canal, gaining a birds-eye view of global trade routes. Such experiences establish an intimacy with global politics that simply isn't feasible with traditional 2D mediums.

Countries' borders and the diverse cultures they enclose can be experienced first-hand employing VR. It instantaneously captures changes in political scenarios, attaching a spatial context to otherwise detached events. Color-coding regions based on political affiliations, simulating historical events, creating 3D models of international crises, all add extraordinary depth to international political education.

VR might even have a role in diplomacy itself. International delegations could use this platform for virtual meetings or mediations, reducing travel time and costs. Immersive experiences in conflict zones could incite empathy and expedite peace negotiations.

3.5. Future Prospects

The appetite for VR technology is growing, and its promise in the geopolitical spectrum is colossal. As technology progresses, so will the depth and fidelity of experiences VR provides. Advancements with AI and machine learning promise even more personalized and enriched virtual experiences.

Additionally, the development and popularization of accessory technologies such as haptic suits and omnidirectional treadmills will elevate experiences from visual and aural to tactile, offering users a multisensory dive into the intricate dance of geopolitics.

In conclusion, VR's potential in the geopolitical world is just beginning to be realized. As we become more adept at using this technology, its influence is set to transform not just our understanding of global politics, but how we interact, empathize, and ultimately, coexist in this world. In our following chapters, we'll delve deeper into specific applications of VR in geopolitics, providing an immersive guide in this fascinating intersection of technology and politics.

Chapter 4. Replicating Borders in the Virtual Sphere

The replication of geopolitical boundaries in a virtual environment introduces a whole new dimension to the understanding of political, social, and economic spaces. It involves transforming 2-dimensional lines of demarcation into vivid, interactive simulations offering a more comprehensive view of these divides.

4.1. Converting 2D Borders to 3D

A critical step in replicating borders in the virtual sphere involves converting 2D representations into 3D. Traditional 2D representations of borders, such as what we find on physical maps or geographical information system (GIS) software, exhibit a limited spatial understanding.

Converting these lines of demarcation into 3D involves a comprehensive analysis of each border's unique features. Each country's form, hinged on its topography, hydrography, and societal factors, takes on a new life in this immersive environment, providing an all-encompassing perspective.

Consider, for instance, the mountainous borders between Nepal and China. They aren't merely lines on a map but colossal, tangible barriers that have shaped interactions between these countries. Rendering these borders in 3D enables users to truly comprehend their scale, helping to offer insight into the unique geopolitical issues that arise in these regions.

4.2. Implementing Real-world Geographies

Creating a virtual geopolitical sphere not only involves recognizing man-made lines of division but also implementing atmospheric scenery and geographical variances like flora, fauna, human settlements, infrastructure, and cultural landmarks that are specific to the region along the border. Treating each border as a living, breathing entity, rather than a static line on a map, offers a truer-to-life portrayal of how borders influence the cultures and economies of the nations they separate.

This can be illuminating, demonstrating how the surrounding geography molds diplomatic relationships. For example, replicating the Amazon rainforest along Brazil's borders might depict the environmental alliances or conflicts between border nations, shedding light on deforestation dilemmas or disputes over natural resource allocation.

4.3. Human Activity Overlay

An important aspect of the replication process is overlaying human activity within the virtual spaces. This involves mapping urban areas, transportation networks, and other traces of human civilization.

For instance, visualizing the heavy industrial activities alongside the Canada-United States border hints at the strong bilateral trade relationship. Observing the sparse settlements along the Russia-China border might offer insights into the colder diplomatic relations.

Human activity overlay also invites opportunities to showcase the cultures and societal norms that exist along border lines, giving a richer understanding of the geopolitical dynamics at play.

4.4. Demarcation of Conflict Zones

A crucial feature of a comprehensive virtual geopolitical sphere is the demarcation of conflict zones. Visualizing disputed territories, militarized areas, or locations of historical unrest can paint an accurate picture of the tense relationships between particular nations.

By rendering these conflict zones in all their stark reality, users can gain an understanding of less visible impacts of borders — how they could incite divisions or heighten nationalist sentiments, or be the cause of economic or humanitarian crises.

4.5. Interactive Engagement

An immersive virtual environment can be made more interactive with the incorporation of data points and user-driven exploration. Users can zoom into regions of interest, engage with embedded indicators to learn specifics about the area or historical event, or layer additional pieces of information such as migration patterns or trade routes to visually correlate data against geopolitical boundaries. Such interactivity fosters a deeper comprehension of complex geopolitical themes.

In conclusion, the journey of replicating borders in the virtual sphere is intricate and multifaceted, merging the realms of geography, history, and politics. This approach makes visible the invisible, offering unique insights into world cultures and international relations. It's an ever-evolving process, reflecting the dynamism and complexity of our real-world geopolitics.

Chapter 5. Virtual Diplomacy: Interactive Experiences of International Relations

In the digital age where virtual reality (VR) has become more accessible, the means and methods for education, information dissemination, and international communication are evolving. As we journey through this new landscape, we first make a stop at historical diplomacy - the traditional representation of international relations.

5.1. Historical Diplomacy: A Primer

Since the dawn of civilization, diplomacy has played an integral role in shaping societies and nations. Diplomacy has roots tracing back to ancient civilizations and is crucial in resolving disputes, forging alliances, making peace, and more. One might imagine ancient diplomats trekking across arid deserts or sailing stormy seas to deliver messages or negotiate treaties. By considering this historical context, we can better appreciate the current, and future shifts in the diplomatic landscape.

Moving from historical diplomacy, our next destination is the digital revolution and its implications for diplomatic practice.

5.2. The Digital Diplomacy Revolution

The advent of the Internet and the digital era caused a seismic shift in diplomacy. Suddenly, distances shrunk, and communication, instant. Information sharing became lightning fast, propelling diplomacy into a completely new realm. Governments, international organizations, and diplomatic entities started leveraging digital platforms to interact, negotiate, and form alliances. Known as digital diplomacy or eDiplomacy, this new mode of operation brought significant change, but nothing compares to the advancements brewing in the realm of virtual reality.

5.3. Virtual Reality: A Paradigm Shift in Diplomatic Practice

VR is poised to completely transform diplomacy. It has the potential to build 'virtual embassies,' a conceptual shift from physical diplomacy to a more inclusive, interactive, and visually tangible platform. Imagine a world where diplomats don't just read about international crises, but are transported to virtual ground zero to witness the reality firsthand. They experience the nuances and embrace the perspectives that were earlier only accessible via text or second-hand accounts. This novel approach promises not only enhanced understanding, but empathy-driven diplomacy—a key ingredient missing from traditional methods.

5.4. Constructing Virtual Embassies

Virtual embassies are spaces that use VR technology to represent a country and its diplomatic mechanisms in the digital world. They can be custom designed and regularly updated to reflect the country's current political climate, culture, and values. From the architectural design reflecting the nation's heritage, viewers can visit virtual galleries filled with historical artifacts, or step into an interactive simulation that explains domestic policies, legislation, and international agreements.

This immersive experience provides a comprehensive understanding of a nation's individuality that goes beyond what a textbook can provide. It gives a new meaning to diplomatic engagement by promoting experiential learning, thus enriching cultural exchanges and awareness.

5.5. The Advent of Virtual Dialogues

While emails, video calls, and social media greatly enhanced communication, virtual dialogues utilizing VR offer a completely different dimension. Diplomats can engage in discussions in a virtual international assembly, experiencing the full semantics of communication, including body language, facial expressions, and spatial positioning. This goes a long way in eliminating misunderstandings and fostering stronger, more transparent international relations.

Imagine diplomats from warring nations transported to a virtual neutral ground— no threat, no physical barriers, pure dialogue. The potential of such virtual dialogues massively increases the prospects of peace negotiations and resolution of international disputes.

5.6. Simulation of Geopolitical Scenarios

With VR, we can simulate geopolitical crises and play out potential scenarios. This method, reminiscent of war games, allows diplomats and decision-makers to evaluate the consequences of their actions in a risk-free environment. In such virtual simulations, the graphics are full-bodied, interaction realistic and the experience, eerily authentic reminding the players the implications of their play in the real world. An assemblage of these factors can ultimately contribute to more informed, wise decision-making in geopolitics.

The journey across the digitally transformed face of diplomacy is certainly intriguing. As we move from physical embassies to virtual ones, from face-to-face dialogues to VR-enabled interactive discussions, and move from risk-ridden geopolitical decisions to virtually simulated outcomes, we are staring at a future where technology determines the course of world peace and war. Yet, this voyage reminds us that the goal remains the same— using every means possible to bridge divides, resolve conflicts, and foster international harmony. Welcome to the future of diplomacy. Enjoy the ride.

Chapter 6. Significant Political Turning Points: A VR Analysis

In the ever-evolving world of global politics, pivotal turning points have irreversibly redrawn borders, reshuffled alliances, and re-ordered world powers. Grasping their magnitude and importance can be daunting, yet Virtual Reality (VR) offers an innovative, immersive approach. By presenting these turning points through the lens of VR, we move beyond static maps and dense texts, making past transitions and their lasting impacts tantalizingly tangible.

6.1. The Mandate System: Geographical Scramble Post World War I

It's hard to overstate the political convulsions following World War I, a convoluted time of territorial exchanges. VR delivers a potent understanding of this period by allowing users to grasp the interplay between bitter negotiations and national ambitions. In a VR reconstruction, you stand in the Palace of Versailles. As you navigate the grand halls, you witness the discussions, the dissent, the elation and despair of world leaders engaged in the creation of a new world order.

The shifting 3D geopolitical lines surface around you. You can touch the new borders being drawn, witnessing the birth of new nations and the disintegration of empires. As you reach out into this virtual space, you trace the progression of the chaotic reorganization, from the assignment of mandates by the League of Nations to the establishment of countries like Iraq and Syria.

6.2. The Yalta Conference: Power Triptych at the End of World War II

World War II, the deadliest conflict in human history, ultimately reshaped international politics. The Yalta Conference forms the centrepiece of this transformation, where decisions taken by three key powers—the United States, the United Kingdom, and the Soviet Union—not only wrapped up the war but also laid the groundwork for the Cold War era.

Imagine yourself in the Livadia Palace, a grand sea-front residence in the Crimean city of Yalta. This VR enactment brings alive the dynamics between Roosevelt, Churchill, and Stalin. See Churchill's stern resolve, Roosevelt's strategic finesse, and Stalin's grim determination. As these giants navigate the ensuing discussions, the post-war borders redraw themselves accordingly, enabling you to visualize East versus West tensions unfolding spatially.

6.3. The Fall of Berlin Wall: A Symbol of Democratic Triumph

Few political events symbolize the victory of liberal democracy on such a massive scale as the fall of the Berlin Wall. Only through VR can one truly understand the scale of this divisive structure. You move along the desolate "death strip", touching the graffitied concrete, feeling the tension, and witnessing the fervor of East Germans as they clamber over the wall amidst jubilant crowds.

Then, the scene shifts. The wall crumbles before you, and in its stead, the Brandenburg Gate emerges, freed from the shadow of the wall. Berlin is unified on the map, and you observe firsthand how the once tense, almost impassable border becomes a free-flowing thoroughfare. Waves of euphoric Germans flood the streets, embodying hope and change as political affiliations rapidly shift around you.

6.4. The Dissolution of the USSR: The Birth of New Nations

As dramatic as it was unexpected, the collapse of the USSR signaled the definitive end of the Cold War order. In this VR exploration, the magnitude of the Soviet dissolution is illuminated. From the Moscow coup attempt to the Belavezha Accords, you're on the ground as these events unfold. You witness the growing dissent in the central Moscow, the glass crack in the iconic Hammer and Sickle symbol, the tension within the Kremlin's walls.

Around you, in the space of the VR environment, the Soviet Union disintegrates, replaced by a mosaic of new independent nations. Watch as economic and political systems metamorphose; see the birth of new governments; follow the recoloring of maps and the redefinition of relationships. Within this immersive setting, the profound geopolitical rifts and subsequent realignments are vividly realized.

Virtual Reality thus presents an unprecedented avenue to explore and comprehend the sprawling panorama of significant political turning points. By offering more than mere proximity, it enables a living understanding of the echoes of history that have cast long-standing impressions on our present geopolitical landscape. We invite you to not only witness the negotiations but participate in this evolving diplomacy, tracing the footprints of world leaders, and realizing how, in their wake, entire nations have been mobilized. Dive into this immersive VR universe, and let fascinating geopolitics unravel organically.

Chapter 7. Demystifying Complex Geopolitical Concepts Through VR

Virtual Reality (VR) is no longer just a gaming or entertainment prop; it has evolved into a serious educational tool, offering immersive experiences that aid in understanding diverse disciplines. Today, we embark on the journey to dive into the role of VR in simplifying the understanding of intricate geopolitical concepts and international relations.

7.1. Understanding Geopolitics

Geopolitics explores the impact of geography on political action and international relations. It is the study of power allocations involving space and territory. The intricate interplay of geographical locations, resources distributions, demographic patterns, historical rivalries, and cultural spheres all combine to create the vast tableau of world politics.

Conceptually, it involves understanding intricate maps, spatial relationships between nations, and the historical contexts that shaped these realities. Traditionally, learning these concepts has been through two-dimensional maps, books, and classroom lectures. However, this only delivers a limited perspective—VR unlocks this limitation, embodying complex geopolitical theories in a 3D environment.

7.2. Virtual Reality: A New Pedagogical Method

Virtual Reality can project 3D geopolitical scenarios that are closer to reality than any textbook variant. Virtual reality creates a world where one can physically visit virtual geopolitical boundaries, seeing first-hand the impact of geographical barriers, trade routes, or resource-rich landscapes on nations and their affairs.

The VR headset is like the wardrobe to Narnia, transcending the conventional approaches to teaching and learning, and exploring concepts as if you're living through them. Its utilitarian value in creating an interactive learning environment fosters cognitive engagement and facilitates the understanding of otherwise abstract geopolitical principles.

7.3. Expanding Spatial Knowledge with VR

Spatial knowledge—the understanding of where things are, the way they are arranged, and how they interconnect—is a crucial part of geopolitics. VR shows promise in enhancing spatial knowledge and understanding. By using VR, students can visit the Ural Mountains that split Europe and Asia, navigate through the Strait of Hormuz, and experience the geopolitical strategic advantage it gives to Iran, or dwell on the vast Siberian planes—often referred to as Russia's natural defense.

Moreover, VR enables students to visualize the impact of physical geography on world affairs in real-time 3D, enhancing their ability to understand and remember spatial relationships between nations.

7.4. Visualizing Political Cartography in 3D

Political maps showing borders, capital cities, key transportation links, etc., are integral to the study of geopolitics. However, 2D representations often lead to an oversimplification of realities, obscuring the actual locales, distances, or terrains shaping geopolitical contexts.

By nature, VR renders three-dimensional models, projecting more accurate representations. Students can traverse borders, fly over capital cities, and note the geographical peculiarities shaping the international relationships of respective nations. VR creates a more holistic, rounded understanding of the world's political landscape—a boon for those seeking to grasp the complexities of geopolitics.

7.5. Illuminating Historical Events and Case Studies

History shapes the present, and the study of geopolitics is no exception. The treaties of Westphalia, Tordesillas, or recent pacts like the Camp David Accords—each of these historical events has sculpted today's world.

Typically, these events and treaties are studied through documents and historiographies. However, VR can recreate these historical moments in immersive simulations. Imagine witnessing the signing of the Treaty of Versailles or the division of Berlin after World War II within a VR environment. Such experiences bring learning to life, turning facts into experiences and fostering a deeper understanding and appreciation of past events.

7.6. Enhancing Comprehension and Retention

Analyzing geopolitical phenomena can be both complex and abstract. One must consider numerous variables—historical, geographical, economic—and their interactions. For many students, these factors provide a complex and challenging learning curve.

Implementing VR in geopolitical education offers an innovative method to help students understand these complex interplays better. This technology facilitates learning by doing—practically applying and experiencing knowledge rather than just theoretically studying it. This approach both enhances the absorption of knowledge and its retention for a longer time, fostering an educated mindset capable of discerning nuanced geopolitical scenarios.

7.7. The Future: Tactical Diplomatic Simulations Through VR

Looking ahead, VR might cater to the training of diplomacy and international relations professionals. Imagine a VR simulation game centered around critical decision-making, inspired by real-world geopolitical situations—negotiating

the Suez Canal crisis or mediating during the Cuban Missile Crisis.

Not only would these simulations serve as training tools for budding diplomats, but they could also help experienced professionals hone their negotiation and decision-making skills. Moreover, constant interaction with such simulations could lead to the development of an instinct for negotiation—something one can only acquire through experience.

In conclusion, VR truly broadens our understanding of geopolitics. Its potential in representing and clarifying complex geopolitical contexts is immense. By remodeling the learning experience, it offers a unique perspective that transcends traditional classroom boundaries. By walking the terrains. witnessing history, and decoding international maneuvers, VR is all set to revolutionize our understanding of geopolitics, one virtual tour at a time.

Chapter 8. Cyber Borders: Mapping Virtual Space

In the modern era, borders have expanded beyond the physical and into the digital realm. This chapter will examine how these so-called "cyber borders"—boundaries within the world wide web—have been formulated and how they are continually redefined by various implications, most crucially politics, law, and technology.

8.1. Evolution and Emergence of Cyber Borders

As the internet took shape in the late 20th century, it was hailed a 'global village,' with the promise of creating a borderless world for information sharing. However, the conception of a borderless internet was often more of an ideal than reality. As the web entwined further into the fabric of society, the lines between physical and digital began to blur, resulting in the formation of cyber borders.

Governments and corporations started creating digital barriers for different purposes, such as protecting sensitive data, maintaining secrecy, and exercising autocratic control over their citizen's online activities. These digital divides, based on jurisdictional boundaries, are reinforced using strategies like IP-based blocking and filtering, and are continually evolving due to geopolitical events, legal precedents, technological advancements, and societal issues.

8.2. Conceptualizing Cyber Borders

Understanding cyber borders requires an appreciation for the fact they are not merely digital replications of physical boundaries. They are, in essence, simultaneously more inclusive and more exclusive.

With the help of geofencing, a strategy that creates a digital perimeter around a real-world geographic area, websites can prohibit access based on the user's location. However, these borders may also be traversed much more easily than their physical counterparts, often requiring no more than a VPN service.

Cyber borders also give rise to new dimensions in geopolitical relations. Big tech companies, for example, can enforce barriers on their platform independently, creating de facto cyber borders. These actions can lead to contentious debates around digital sovereignty, or the internet equivalent of a country's right to govern itself.

8.3. Politics and Cyber Borders

Politics plays a significant role in shaping cyber borders, molding the virtual terrains, just as it does in the physical world. Countries limit access to foreign digital information sources to control the narrative within their borders and maintain political stability. The Chinese 'Great Firewall,' for example, censors international social networks like Facebook and Twitter, while promoting domestic equivalents.

Cyber borders are also drawn due to comprehensive state-sanctioned surveillance programs, where the collection and storage of citizens' online activities are justified under the premise of national security. The revelations by Edward Snowden about PRISM—a clandestine surveillance program run by the United States National Security Agency—highlight how high the stakes can be when traversing these digital divides.

8.4. Legal Implications of Cyber Borders

The legal implications of cyber borders concern not only privacy but also jurisdiction and responsibility. Judicial reach remains one of the main challenges in the digital space, as the transnational nature of the internet clashes with nation-state-centered legal systems. The gradual emergence of cloud computing has further complicated these situations, with data diffused over multiple locations, leading to questions about jurisdiction and accountability.

Moreover, the patent and copyright law landscape is also significantly affected. The geo-blocking of content due to licensing agreements leads to patchwork accessibility to digital products and services across the globe. It's a perfect example of how legal paradigms can influence the makeup of cyber borders.

8.5. Impact of Technology on Cyber Borders

Technological advancements regularly redefine the landscape of cyber borders, rendering them both harder to enforce and to evade. Encryption technologies like VPNs have made it possible to bypass cyber borders, creating a virtual tunnel to another part of the internet world.

On the other hand, advancements in IP tracking, digital watermarking, and AI-based content policing have allowed authorities and corporations to enforce stricter borders. For instance, streaming platforms like Netflix deploy sophisticated mechanisms to block VPN users to uphold regional content licensing.

8.6. Cyber Borders: A Paradox

In summary, cyber borders can be thought of as a paradox. On the one hand, they restrict access, create division and fragmentation on what was thought to be a global stage for unrestricted information exchange. But on the other hand, they can protect intellectual property, uphold law and order, and preserve national security and cultural integrity.

As we continue to journey through our interconnected world, it remains critical to understand the nature and implications of these virtual lines of demarcation. As we have seen, they are as complex and political as their terrestrial counterparts, opening a whole new horizon for global diplomacy and international relations in the digital age.

This is just the beginning of the conversation about how we navigate these cyber borders—these unseen but felt boundaries— and how we can turn digital divides into bridges for understanding, empathy, and cooperation in the networked world.

Chapter 9. The Future of Politics: Simulated Policy Debates

The incorporation of Virtual Reality (VR) in various sectors of human life has heralded a new era where interaction and comprehension of complex subjects become vivid and immersive. This is no less true when it comes to visualizing geopolitical landscapes, international relations, and political discourses. The realm of policy debates and public policy formation could benefit immensely from this revolutionary technology. This chapter unveils the future of political policy debates in a simulated environment, and the delineation of its feasibility and implications.

9.1. The Virtual Arena: Conceptualizing Simulated Policy Debates

The function of a simulated environment in policy discussions can be robust and varied. It could serve as a platform where policy makers, legislators, or other interested parties can come together to discuss, ideate, negotiate, and even vote on policies in real-time. As it creates a sense of presence, VR enables users to interact with data visualizations and engage in comprehensive discussions, eliminating the barriers of geographical distance and time.

Not just confined to domestic policy debates, this technology can also enhance international dialogues and diplomatic negotiations. The immersive VR environment can provide stakeholders with insights into the effects of their decisions on different regions. It can vividly visualize demographic changes, economic impacts, or environmental consequences, thus offering a compelling look into the possible outcomes policy changes can bring about.

9.2. Unwrapping the Power of Policies: A Virtual Dissection

Breaking down complex policies into comprehensible, dissectible, and interactive modules is key when it comes to understanding the associations between individual provisions and overall outcomes. The presentation of policies within a VR-based policy debate will not only immerse members in the conversation but also create a thoughtfully visualized chain of effects.

Imagine a live, multiuser simulation where analysts dive into a proposed healthcare policy. Participants can visually explore different policy scenarios, seeing potential effects in clear terms—increased availability in rural areas, the reduction of medical errors, or the burden on taxpayers, for instance. Through this kind of comprehensive view, legislators can better understand a policy before voting on its implementation.

9.3. A Stage for Citizens: Democratizing Policy Debates

Beyond lawmakers, VR has the potential to democratize policy debates by providing a platform to citizens. People can be given the chance to voice their opinions, vote on proposals, or merely attend to listen, live stats showing participant sentiment. By involving ordinary citizens in these high-level discussions, we not only leverage the collective intelligence of the public but we also promote transparency in decision-making processes.

Simulations can recreate situations that allow citizens to better understand the implications of policy proposals on their lives. These

VR-enabled practices can generate a more informed public that is not just passive spectators but active participants in the policy-making process.

9.4. Digitizing Legislations: A Walkthrough Reality

The enablement of VR in policy discussions also means digitizing legislations to a large extent. Converting conventional texts into a spatial representation not only enables easy visualization of policies, but it also makes the readability of lengthy documents less tedious, thus encouraging comprehensive understanding and expedited decision-making.

However, the effective implementation of VR in policy discussions represents a vast digital transformation undertaking. It would require resources, intensive training, and most importantly, changes in traditional bureaucratic procedures.

9.5. The Road Ahead: Challenges and Possibilities

As we envision the significance of VR in future policy debates, we must also discuss the challenges. Broad-based access to VR technology, data privacy concerns, and equitable representation are potential obstacles that need to be addressed. We need to ensure that the technology does not exacerbate the digital divide; instead, it should bridge that divide, bringing more voices to the table.

Efficient digital policy-making strategies would require real-time updating systems and reliable data sourcing. As simulations rely heavily on the authenticity of data for accuracy, regular monitoring for credibility is pivotal. Moreover, to make VR a universally accepted norm, nations will need to establish standardized digital platforms compatible with global systems, ensuring everyone can 'meet' in the virtual world.

Amid all the implications discussed, the possibilities are endless, limited only by our collective imagination. Implementing simulated policy debates means taking a giant leap in digital governance, potentially revolutionizing political discourse, legislative efficiency, and public engagement on a global scale.

By acknowledging virtual reality's potential and working to overcome its challenges, we can not just modernize, but revolutionize the future of politics. Undeniably, the future of simulated policy debates is not just appealing—it is an impending reality. It may influence democracy's trajectory and alter how we comprehend, navigate, and negotiate geopolitical landscapes in the years to come.

Chapter 10. Social Implications of Virtual Reality in Geopolitics

Virtual Reality (VR) is no longer just a speculative niche of the tech industry; it has evolved into a transformative tool that is redefining how we visualize and comprehend complex systems like geopolitics. This chapter aims to unravel the wide-ranging social implications of utilizing VR in the realm of international relations, both the opportunities it presents and the challenges it engenders.

10.1. The Democratization of Geopolitical Information

One of the primary advantages VR brings to the geopolitical table is the democratization of information. Historically, understanding international politics involved relying heavily on information distilled by experts, often presented in ways less accessible to laypeople. VR technology leaps over this hurdle, enabling a more comprehensive engagement with geopolitics regardless of one's prior knowledge or education.

Visualizing complex geopolitical landscapes, border tensions, and diplomatic strategies in a 3D, interactive format makes it easier for audiences to comprehend. Presenting this spatial, immersive experience can foster greater public awareness and understanding of geopolitical scenarios. The implications of this enhanced global awareness can significantly influence everything from voting behaviors in democratic societies to the public's ability to keep their governments in check.

10.2. Reimagining Educational Landscapes

The use of VR in teaching geopolitics could revolutionize educational methods and contribute significantly to students' understanding of international politics. With VR, one no longer needs to struggle interpreting dense textbooks or static maps to understand international relations. Here, history comes alive, borders become lifelike instead of mere outlines, international conflicts gain tangible contexts, and the web of interconnections between nations is visualized like never before.

Moreover, VR technology cuts across cultural and language barriers. The ability for students of varying ages and cultural backgrounds to collectively engage in real-time virtual experiences can tear down scholastic disparities and draw students closer to a global community.

10.3. Threats to Privacy and Security

However, as with most groundbreaking technologies, the application of VR in geopolitics brings its own set of challenges, the most vital of which concerns privacy and security. It is now possible for State and non-State actors to exploit the technology and present distorted geopolitical information in a bid to drive particular narratives or disinformation campaigns. Furthermore, given the immersive and believable nature of VR, such disinformation could have potent impact.

Moreover, as VR platforms store information about users' behaviors, preferences, and interactions, they could become prime targets for data breaches and cyber attacks, leading to serious privacy and security concerns.

10.4. Ethical Interrogations

The adaptation of VR brings to light various ethical issues as well. On one hand, virtual reality's power to make users feel present in different scenarios can generate more empathetic and informed global citizens. On the other, it raises ethical questions about the nature of 'virtual' reality itself and its impact on users' cognition and perception.

Careful thought must be given to which historical events, border conflicts, or diplomatic incidents are chosen for VR representation and the way these are portrayed. These decisions could subtly impact users' understanding and feelings towards countries, cultures, and political situations, influencing their real-world political standpoints and actions.

10.5. The Digital Divide

The integration of VR in geopolitics also necessarily spawns questions of accessibility. Not everyone around the world has equal access to the Internet, let alone cutting-edge technology such as VR. This disparity raises concerns about the so-called 'digital divide'—the gap between those populations that have access to modern information technology and those that don't—and its impact on understanding and engaging with geopolitics. Efforts must be undertaken to ensure that this revolutionary way of visualizing geopolitics doesn't become another tool contributing to global disparities but instead bridges the gap.

In conclusion, while VR holds the potential to democratize and transform the understanding of geopolitical information, the challenges it presents cannot be dismissed lightly. The successful and ethical integration of VR into geopolitics calls for comprehensive plans that address the digital divide, constructive international policies governing its use, and robust security frameworks to counter potential threats. This, combined with societal awareness and understanding of these dynamics, means that VR's promise in geopolitics may yet be achieved, marking a stepping stone towards a more informed, connected, and empirically comprehensive world.

Chapter 11. Case Studies: Successful Integrations of VR in Geopolitics

In analyzing the role of virtual reality (VR) in the complex world of geopolitical landscapes, a study of its successful integrations is crucial. By spotlighting a collection of captivating examples of VR applications in geopolitics, this chapter showcases the transformative capacity of this immersive technology, enabling a more profound, comprehensive understanding of political dynamics slicing across global spectrums. Various case studies reveal how VR ensures the visualization of geopolitical scenarios, bringing abstract concepts to life—all the while offering a novel entry point into understanding and negotiating our world's intricate political maze.

11.1. Adoption by United Nations

Noted for its pioneering approach towards technology, the United Nations (UN) is one of the earliest adopters of VR in the geopolitical landscape. Specifically, the UN initiated a Virtual Reality Series to bring global diplomatic leaders within the unseen realms of crisis-stricken zones. By embodying the experiences of people living through crises, from Syrian refugees to climate change victims, VR technology allowed diplomats to transcend the usual barriers of distance and disconnection, fostering empathy and possibly influencing diplomatic decisions on crucial matters.

The VR project named "Clouds Over Sidra" by the UN is a fitting example. The project offered insights into the life of Sidra, a 12-year-old Syrian girl in the Za'atari camp in Jordan. Using VR, decision-makers experienced first-hand her daily experiences, making the distant crisis more tangible and real, which consequently had substantial impacts on discussions at humanitarian conferences, influencing fund allocations and policy design.

11.2. Advancements in Virtual Diplomacy

Digital diplomacy, particularly virtual diplomacy, has entered the political radars of multiple nations. Virtual embassies are gaining popularity as a means of assisting global communication and conflict resolution processes, employing VR technology to simulate diplomatic situations and engage in training programs or diplomacy exercises.

One such example is the Virtual Embassy program initiated by the U.S. The program uses virtual reality to create a constructive platform for information exchange and communication between ambassadors or diplomats of different nations. The VR environment allows participants to negotiate, strategize, and resolve issues, replicating the dynamics of real-life diplomacy.

When the U.S. embassy in Iran was shut down, a virtual space stood in its stead, providing services such as visa applications and cultural exchange—ensuring some level of diplomatic engagement despite strained relations.

11.3. Educational Approach: Stanford's Virtual Humanities Lab

Recognizing the educational potential of VR, Stanford University established the Virtual Humanities Lab, using VR in creating detailed, immersive historical reconstructions—for instance, recreating a World War II setting to enable the exploration of the geopolitical implications of the war.

The experience provided by VR allowed users to understand the severity of the war in a vicarious manner. By creating treacherous battlegrounds and war-torn cityscapes, VR demonstrated the terrifying reality and the environmental degradation war entails. Overall, this immersive exercise contributed significantly towards an expanded comprehension of the geopolitical shifts during and after the war.

11.4. Role in Resolving Border Disputes

At the intersection of border disputes and technology, VR presents a fascinating solution—virtual borders—and their potential as conflict resolution tools are being explored.

An instance of this is visible in the ongoing border dispute between India and Pakistan over the region of Kashmir. A non-profit, based in the UK, leveraged VR to create virtual borders—they assembled a VR representation of the contentious Line of Control, symbolizing the disputed border between the two countries, thereby making the contentious issue accessible to the broader public geographically and conceptually.

While such projects are not expected to resolve long-standing disputes, they can serve as a starting point, opening new dialogues and perspectives, and hopefully ushering in pathways for negotiations and solutions.

11.5. Summary

These case studies, alongside numerous others, confirm the transformative potential of VR in different facets of geopolitics—from the UN's heart-wrenching depictions of worldwide crises, Stanford University's immersive curriculum, constructing virtual embassies for international relations, and digital visualization of disputed land.

VR applications have demystified the geopolitical panorama, and although optimal integration continues to be navigated—it is irrefutable that VR holds a future in geopolitics, disrupting traditional paradigms. To further its potential, we need to focus on innovation and accessibility, ensuring this powerful tool is harnessed to its utmost capacity for global harmony.

www.ingramcontent.com/pod-product-compliance
Lightning Source LLC
Chambersburg PA
CBHW062307290526
45794CB00006B/2715